CONSTRUCTION

Coloring Book For Kids!

A Unique Collection Of Coloring Pages

Bold Illustrations
COLORING BOOKS

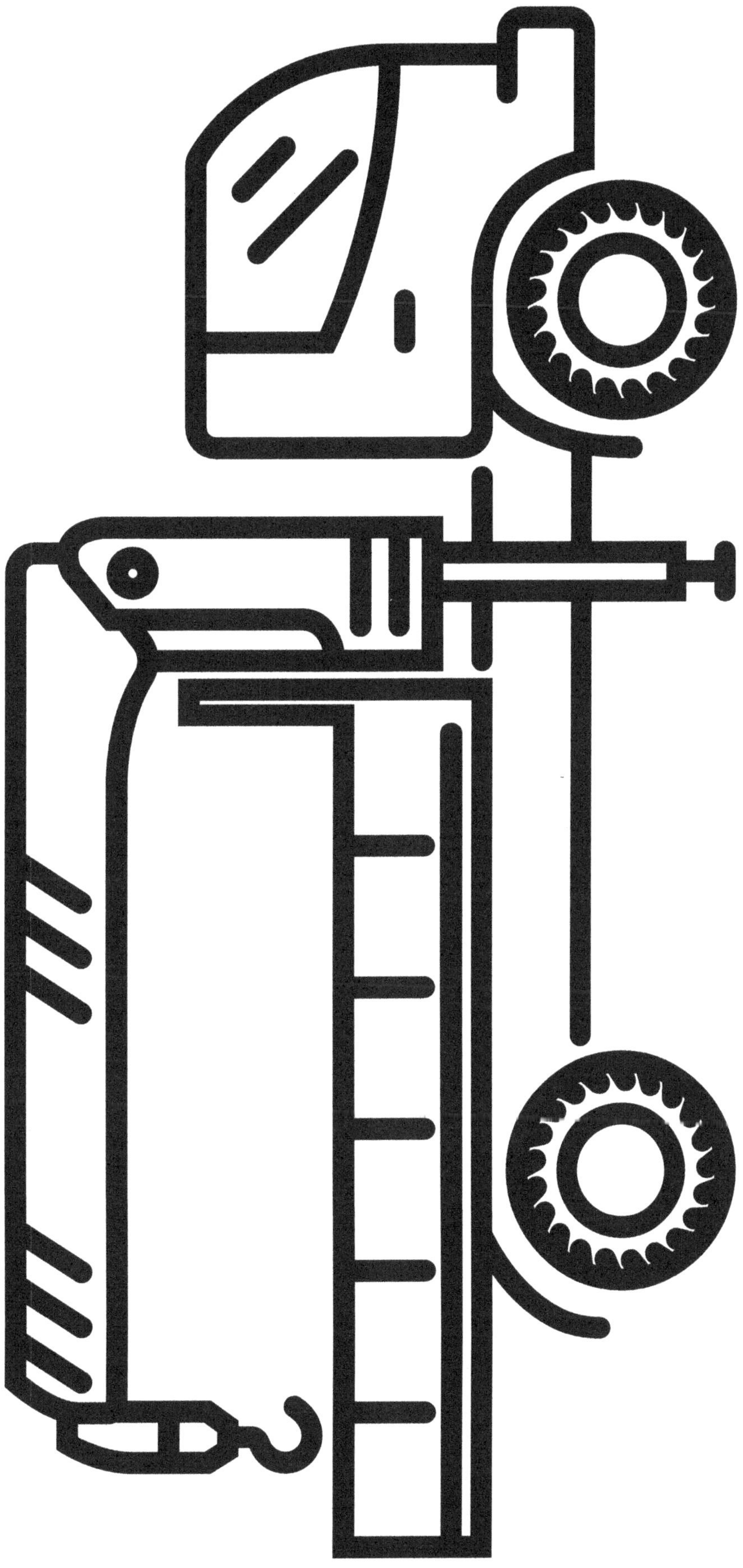

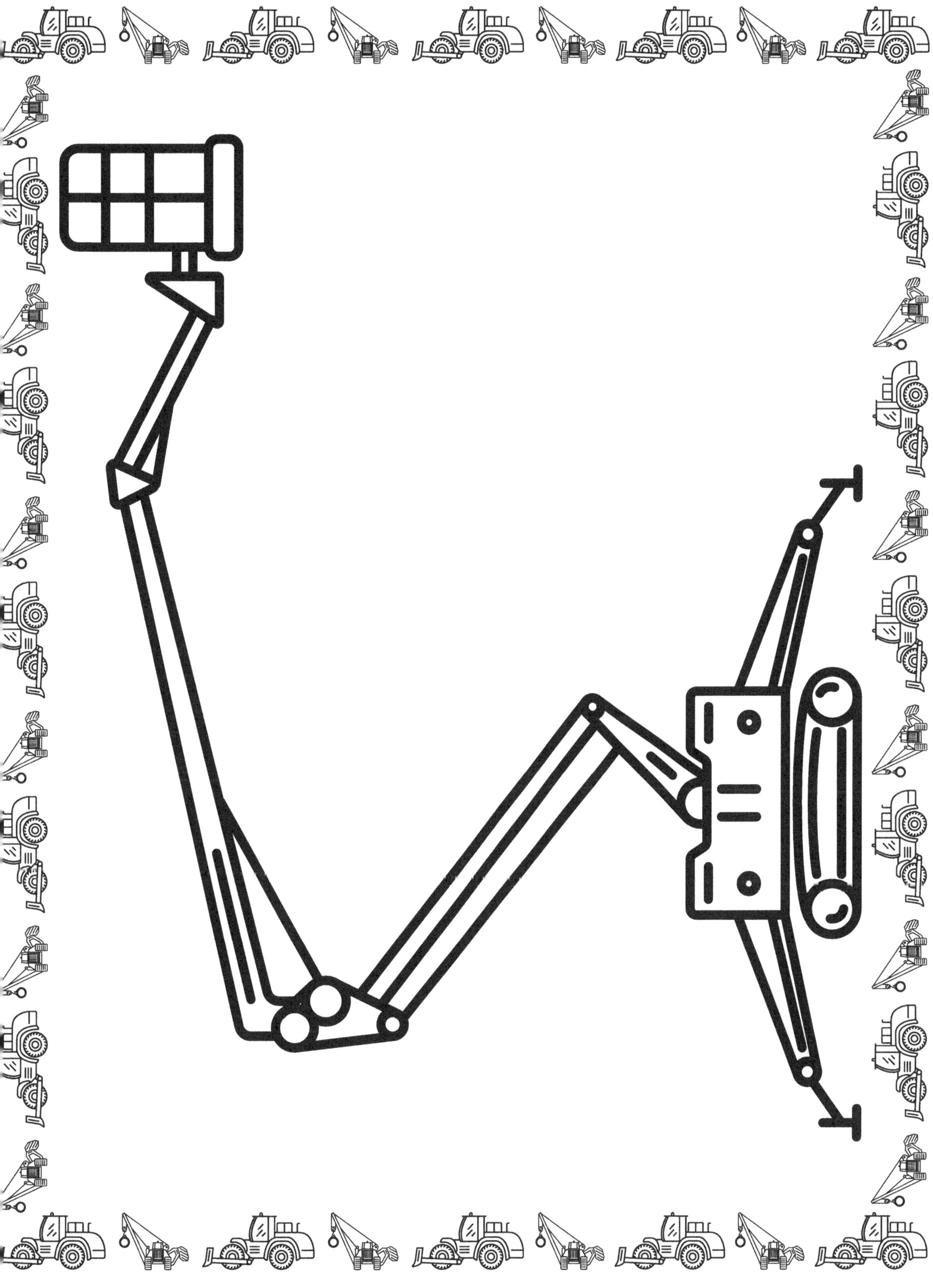

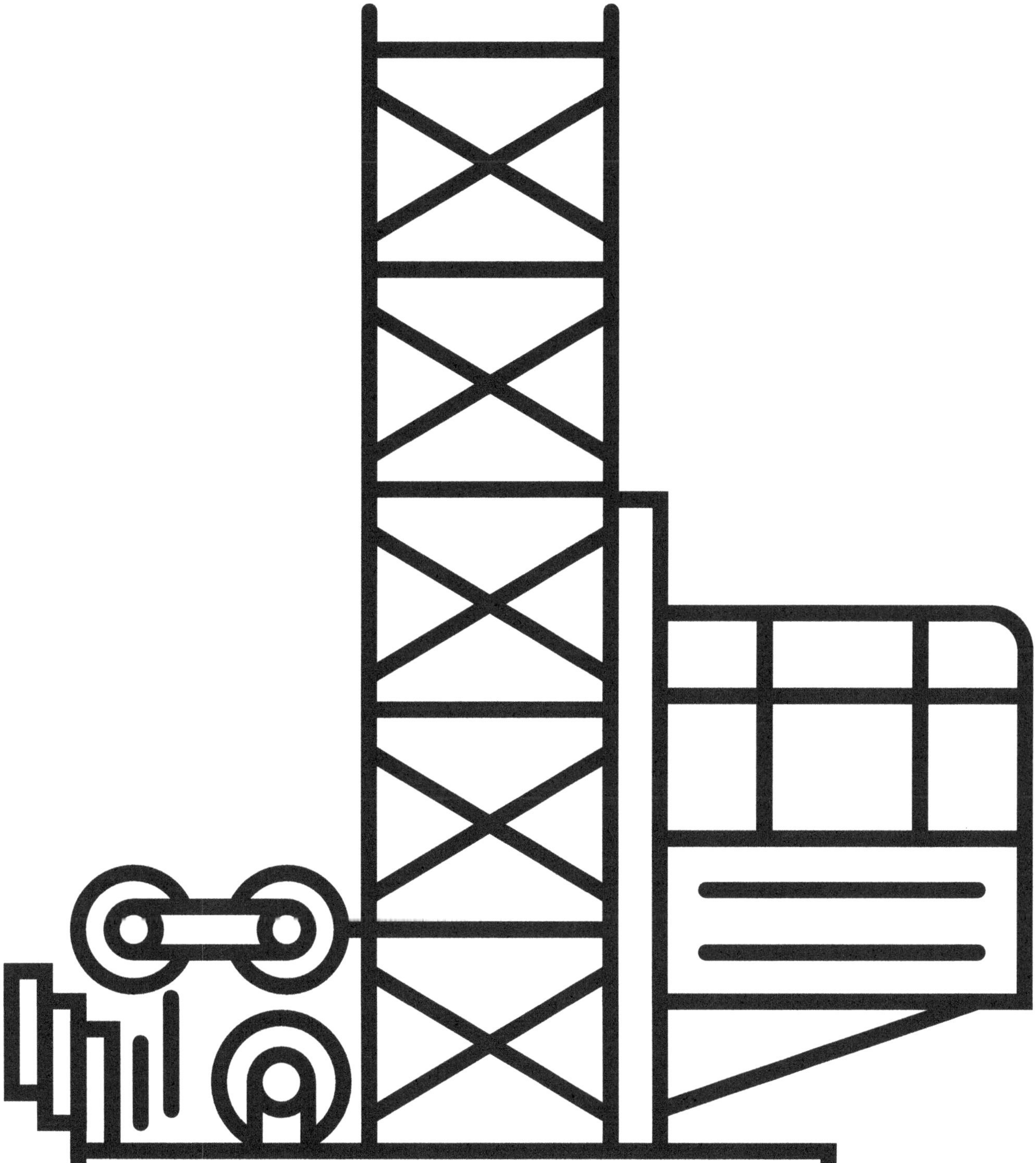

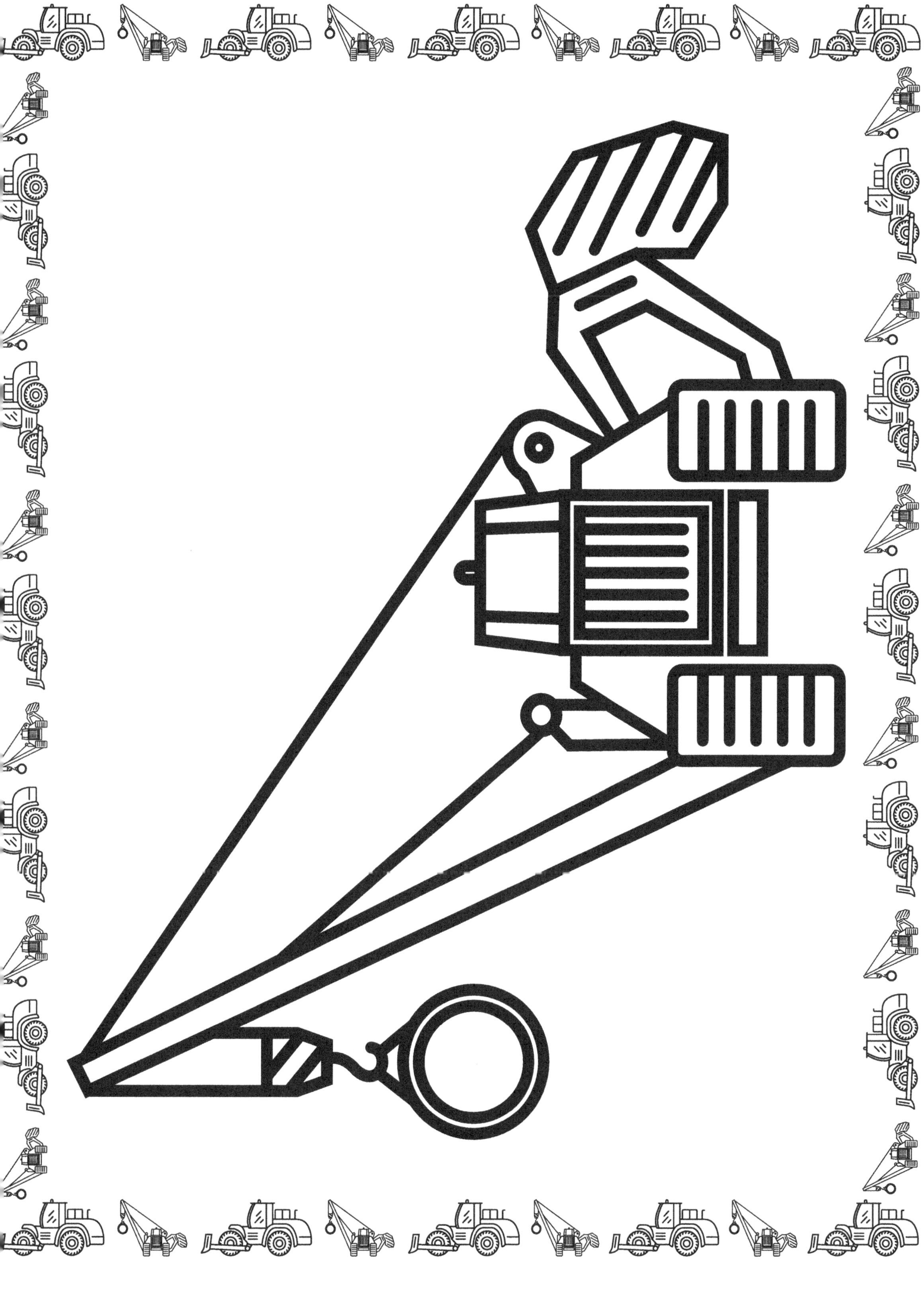

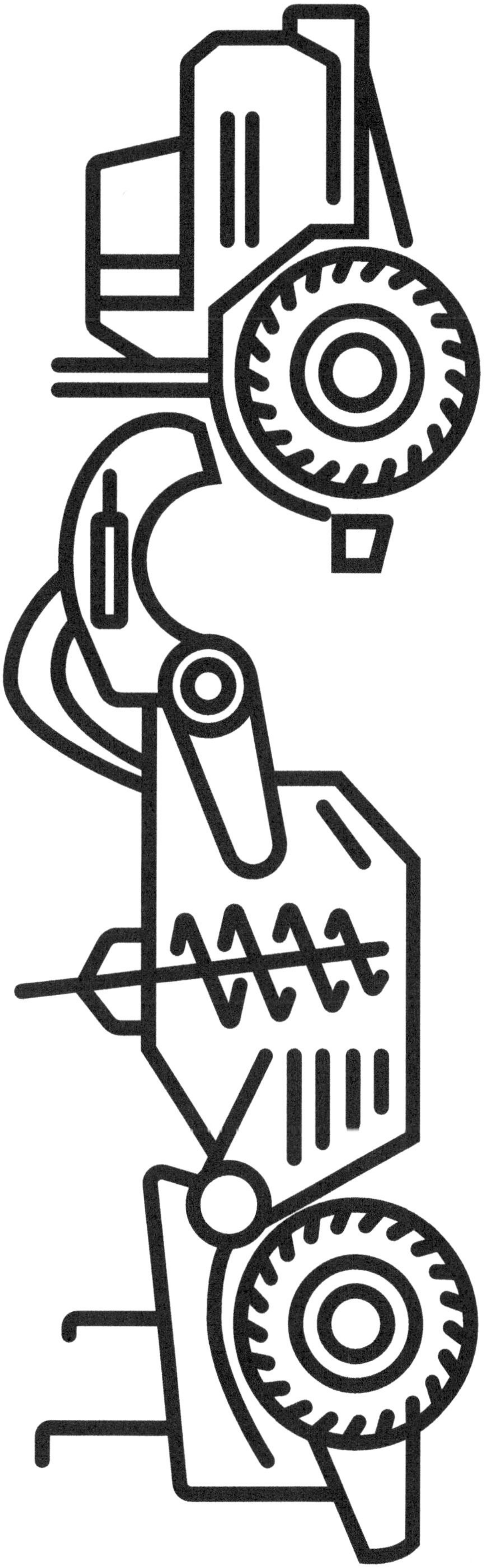

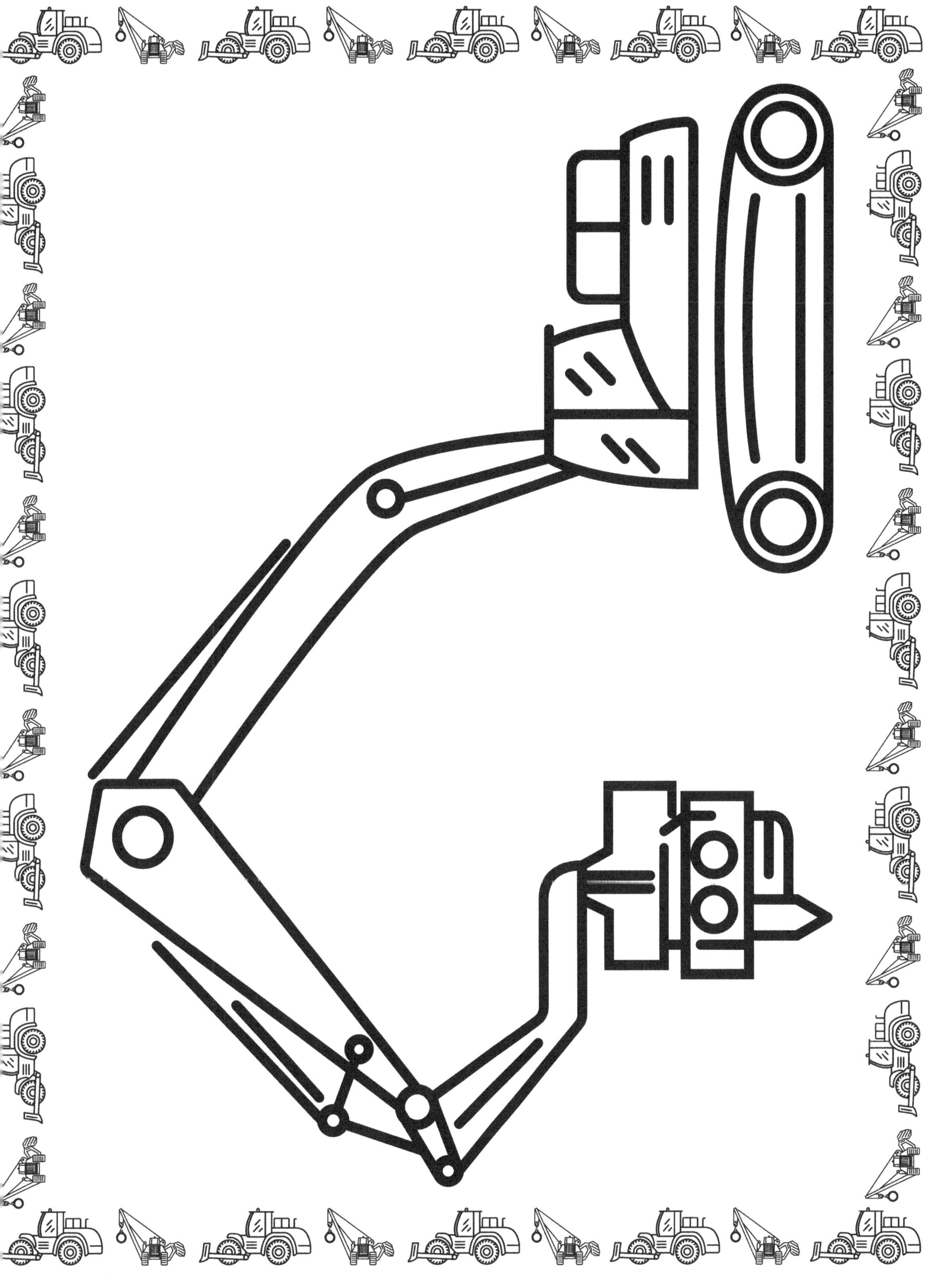

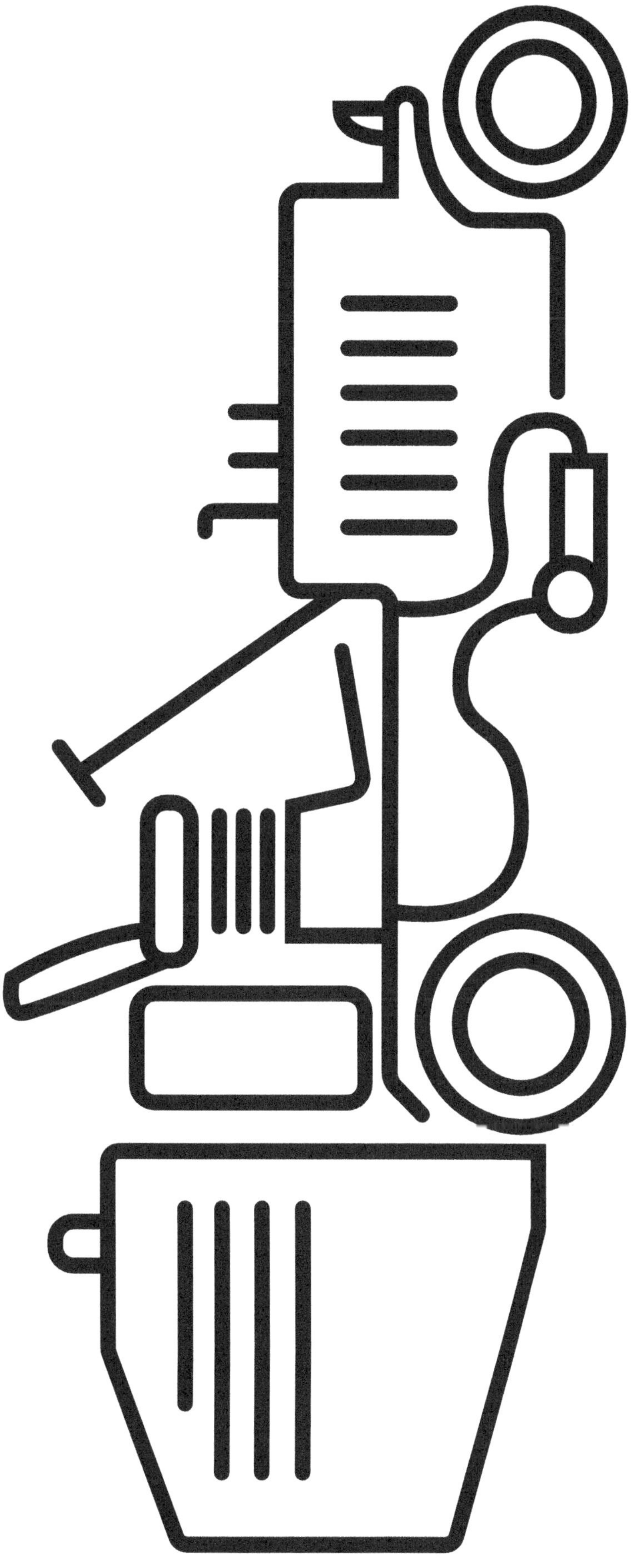

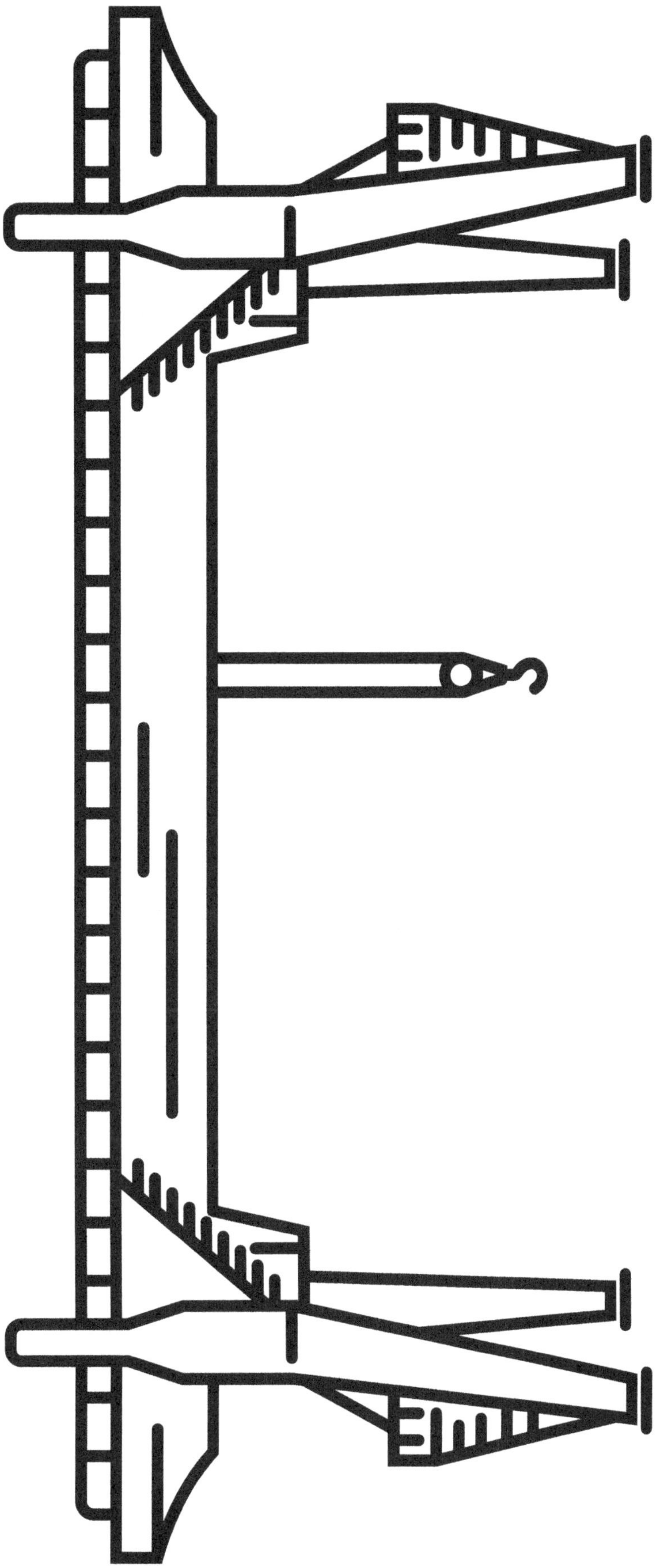

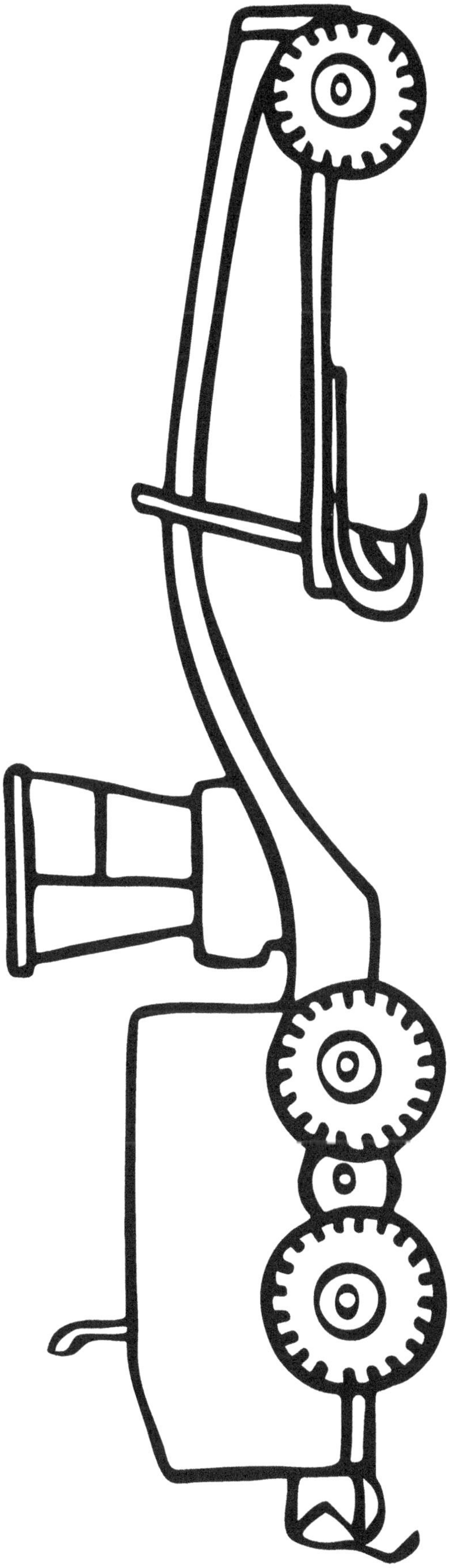

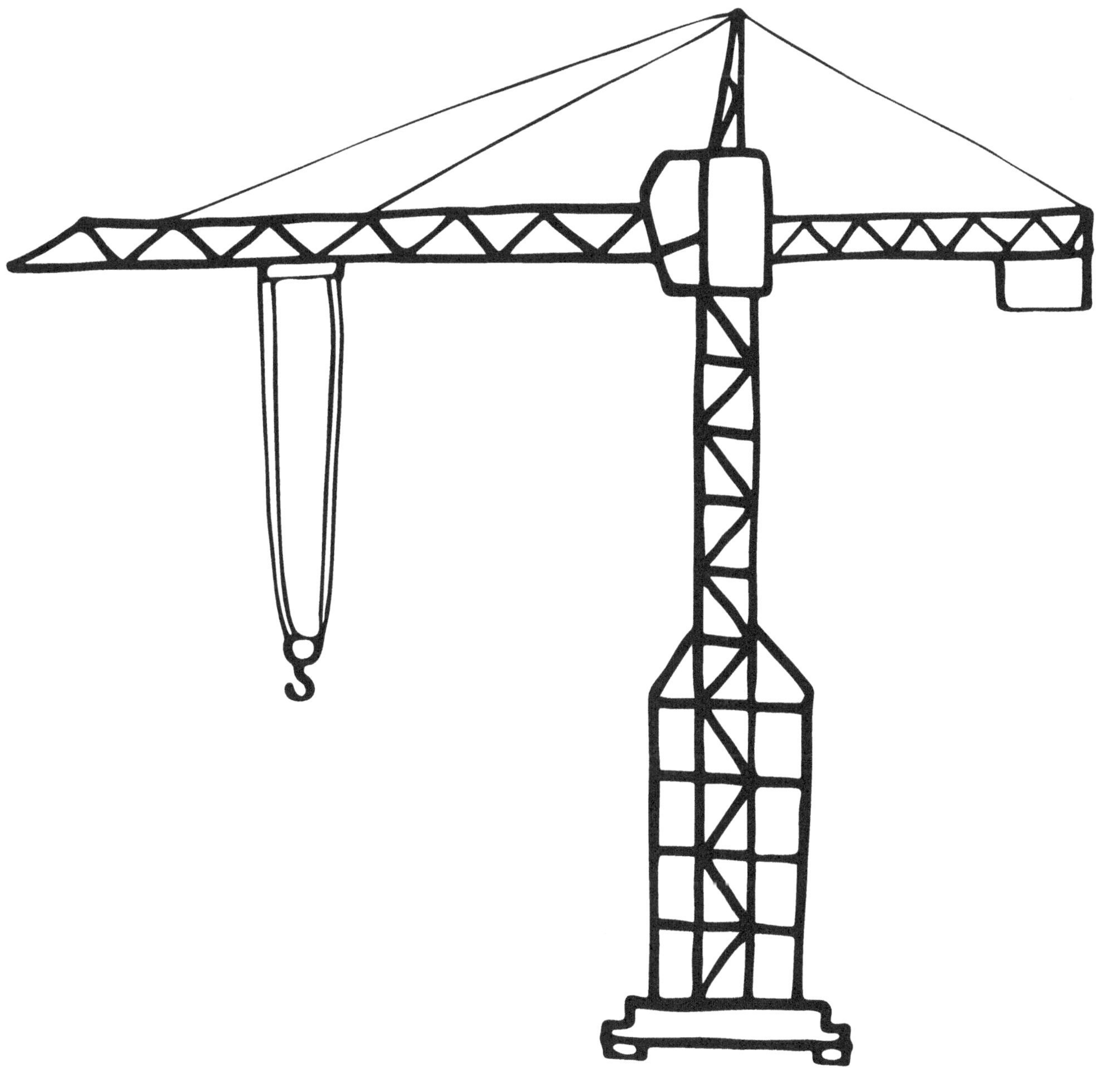

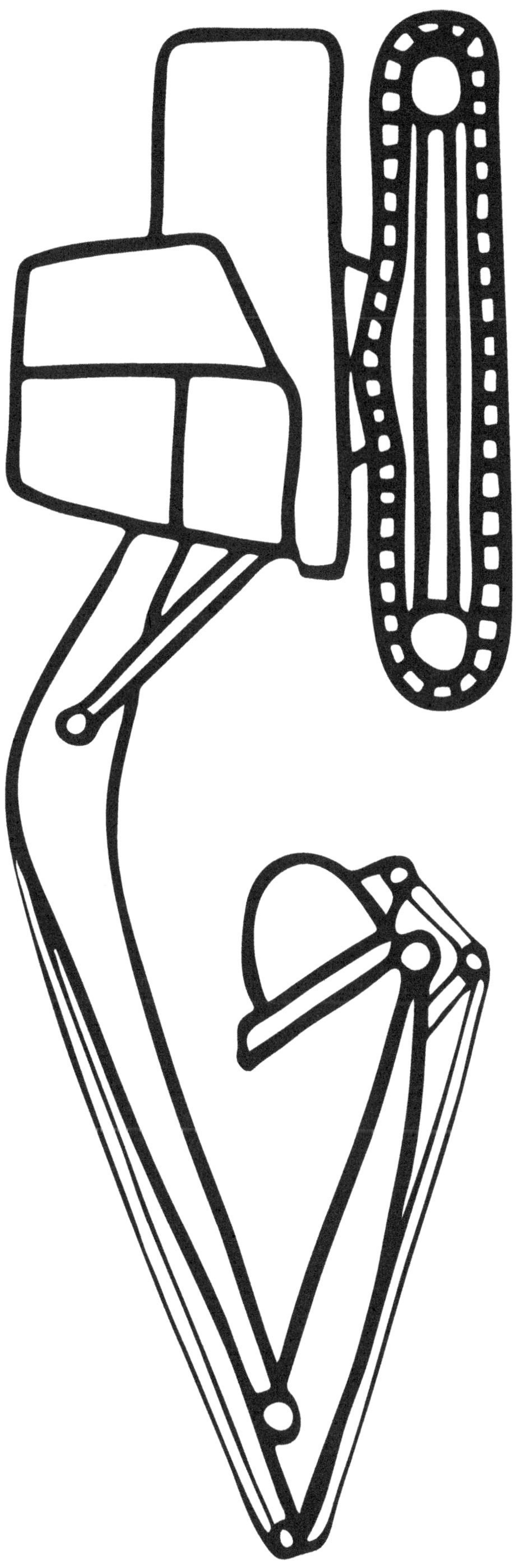

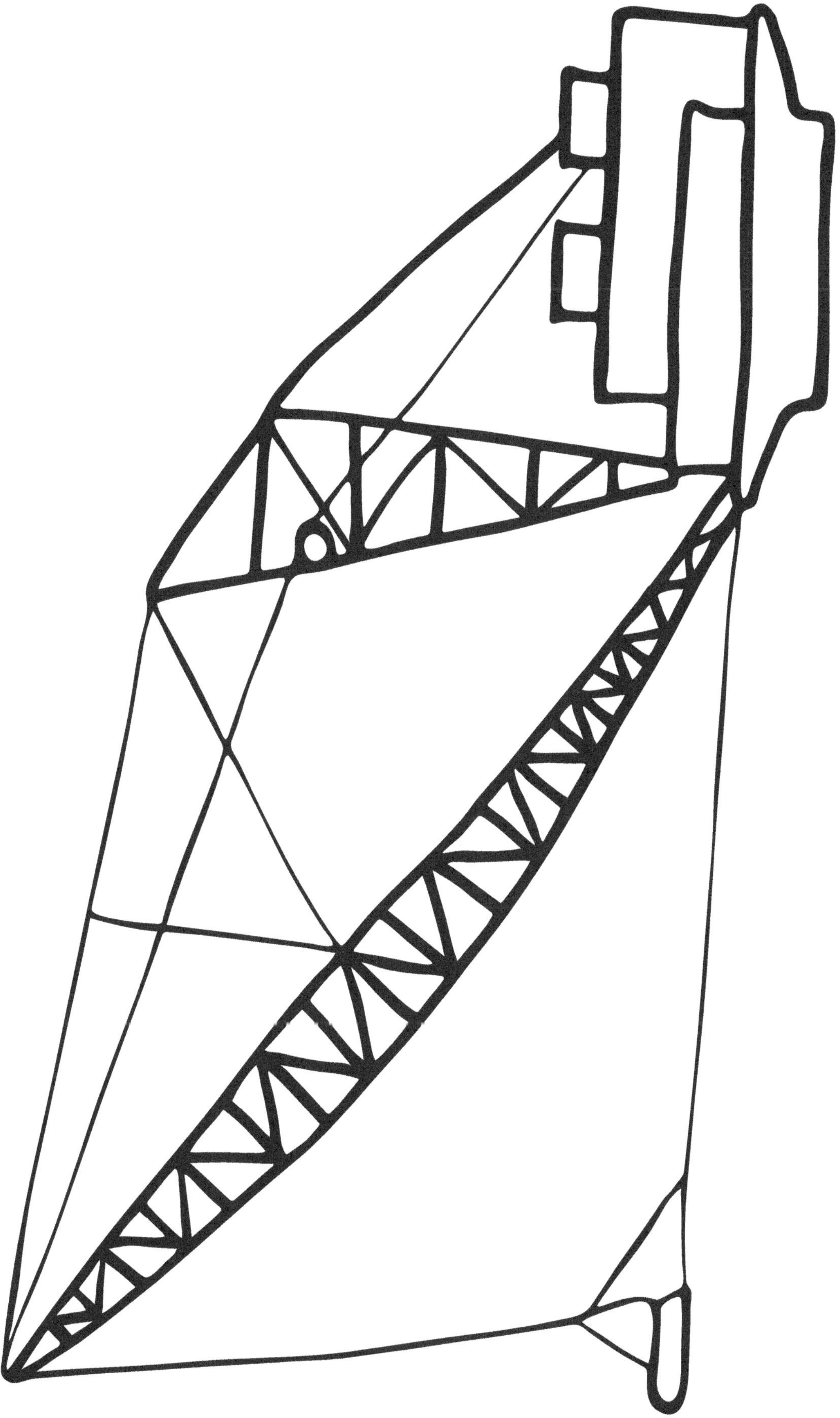

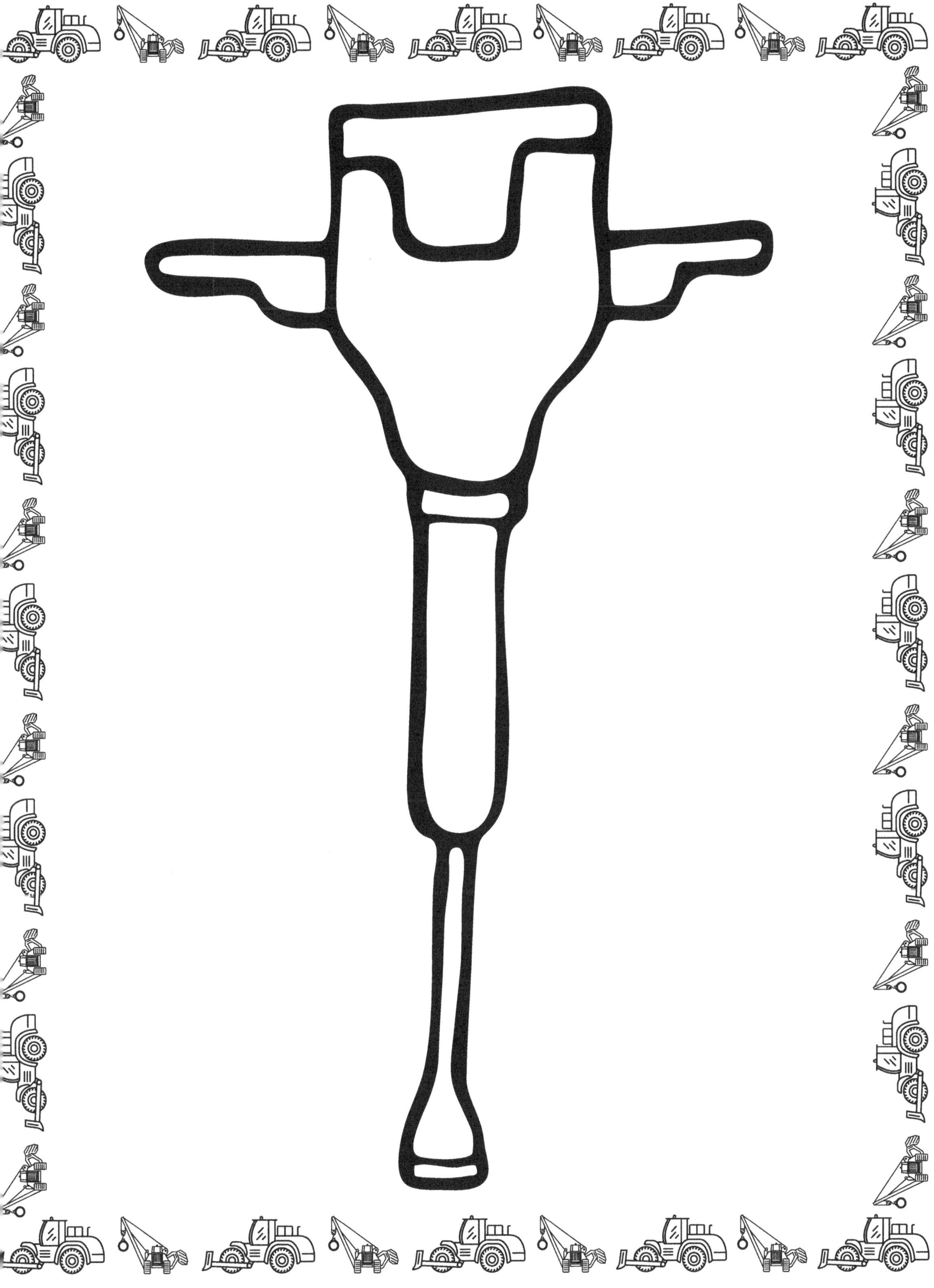

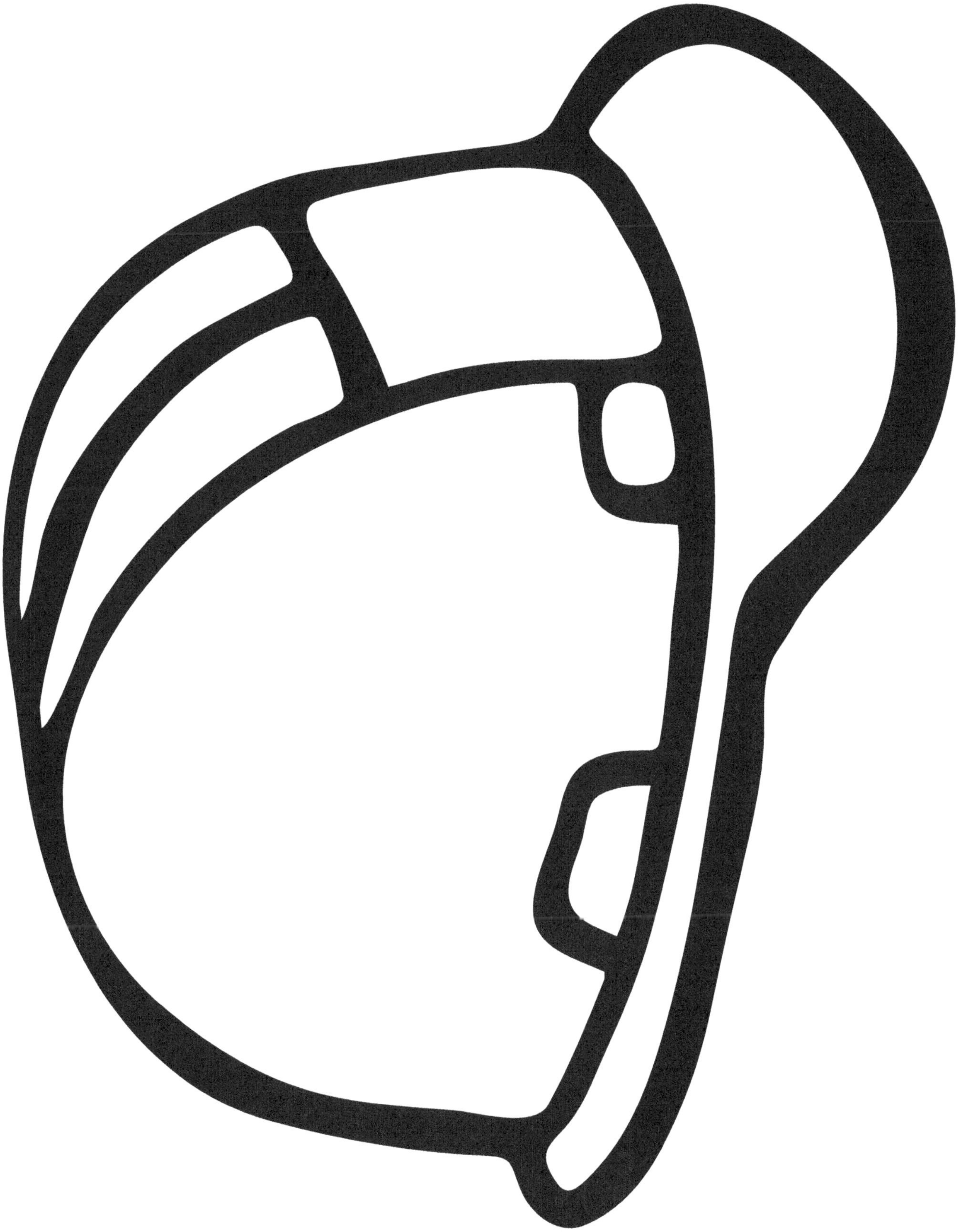

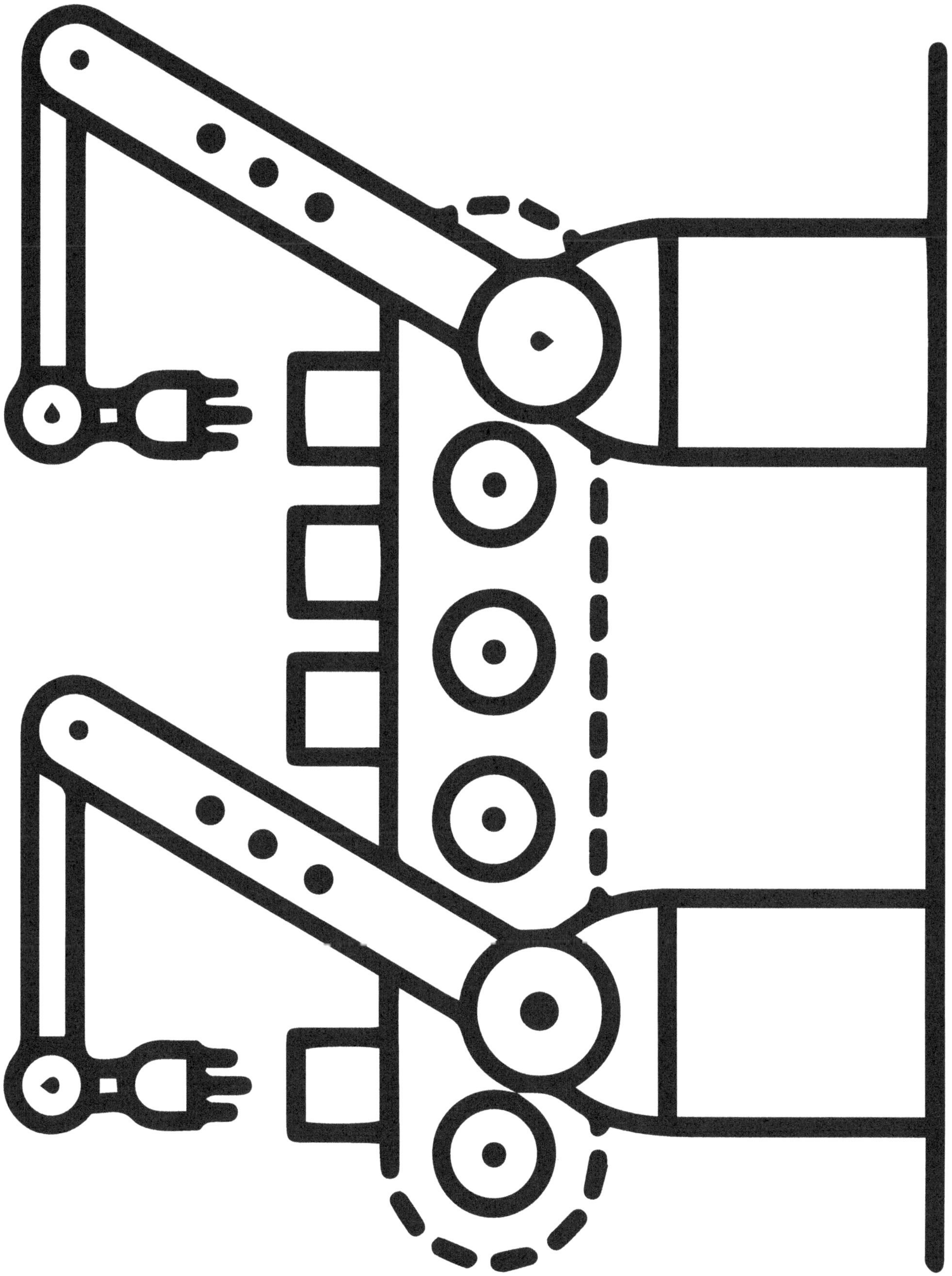

This is a Bleed Through Page If You Are Using a Colouring Marker or Pen!

Find Other Great Titles By searching for Bold Illustrations on Your Favorite Book Retailer

Amazon.Ca | Barnes & Noble (BN.Com) | Books A Million (BAM.Com)

Bold Illustrations

COLORING BOOKS

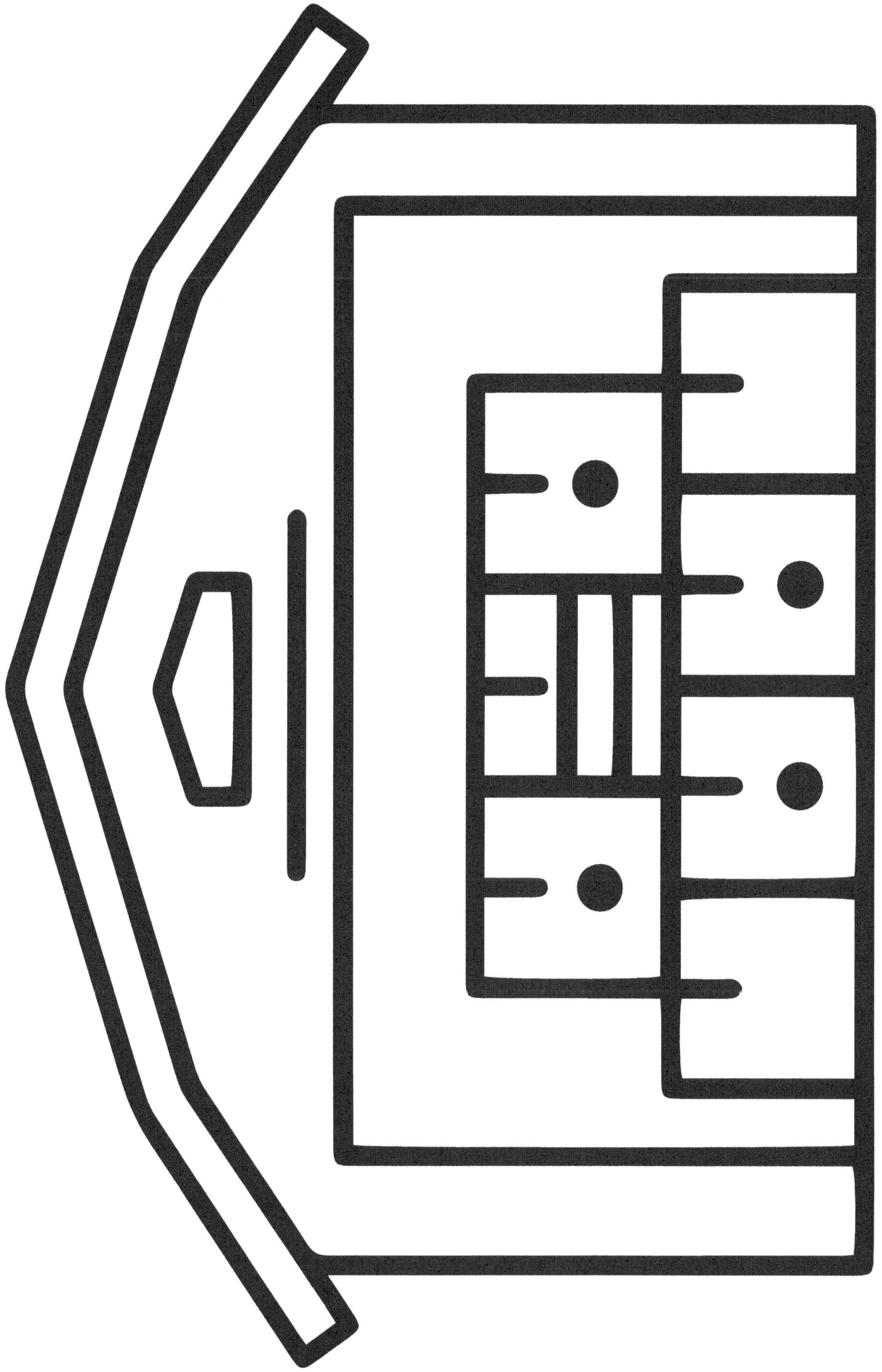

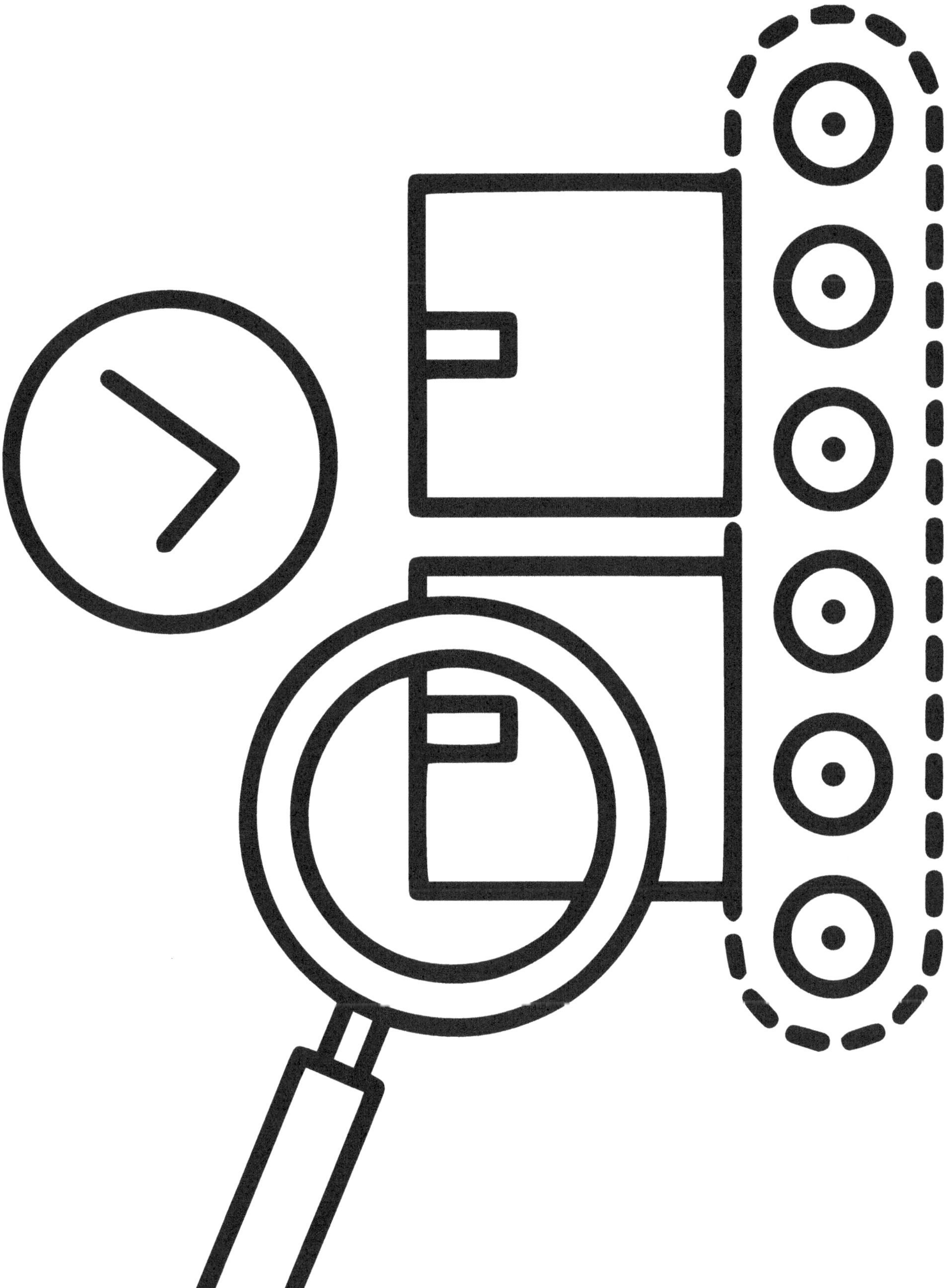

This is a Bleed Through Page If You Are Using a Colouring Marker or Pen!

Find Other Great Titles By searching for Bold Illustrations on Your Favorite Book Retailer

Amazon.Ca | Barnes & Noble (BN.Com) | Books A Million (BAM.Com)

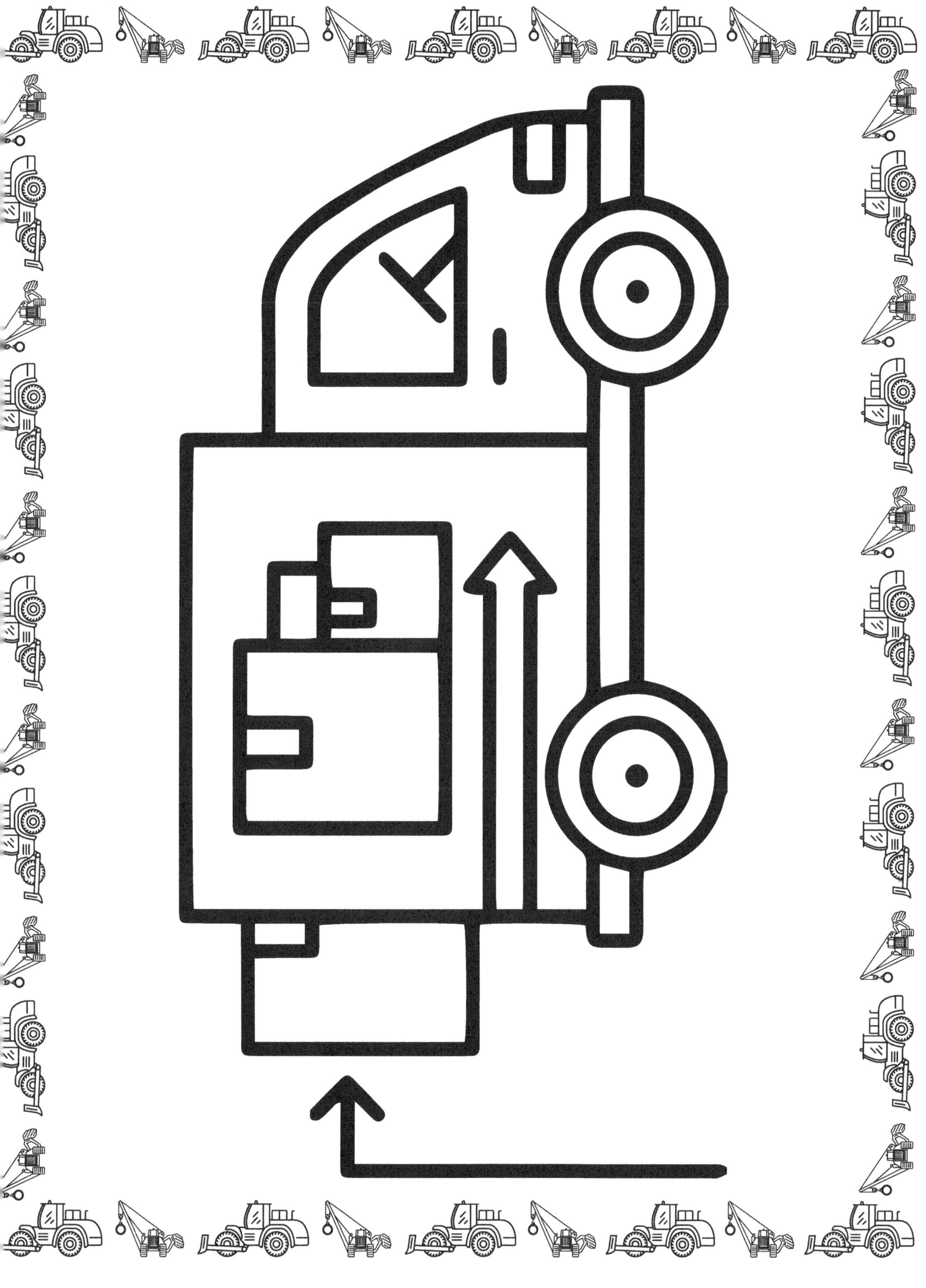

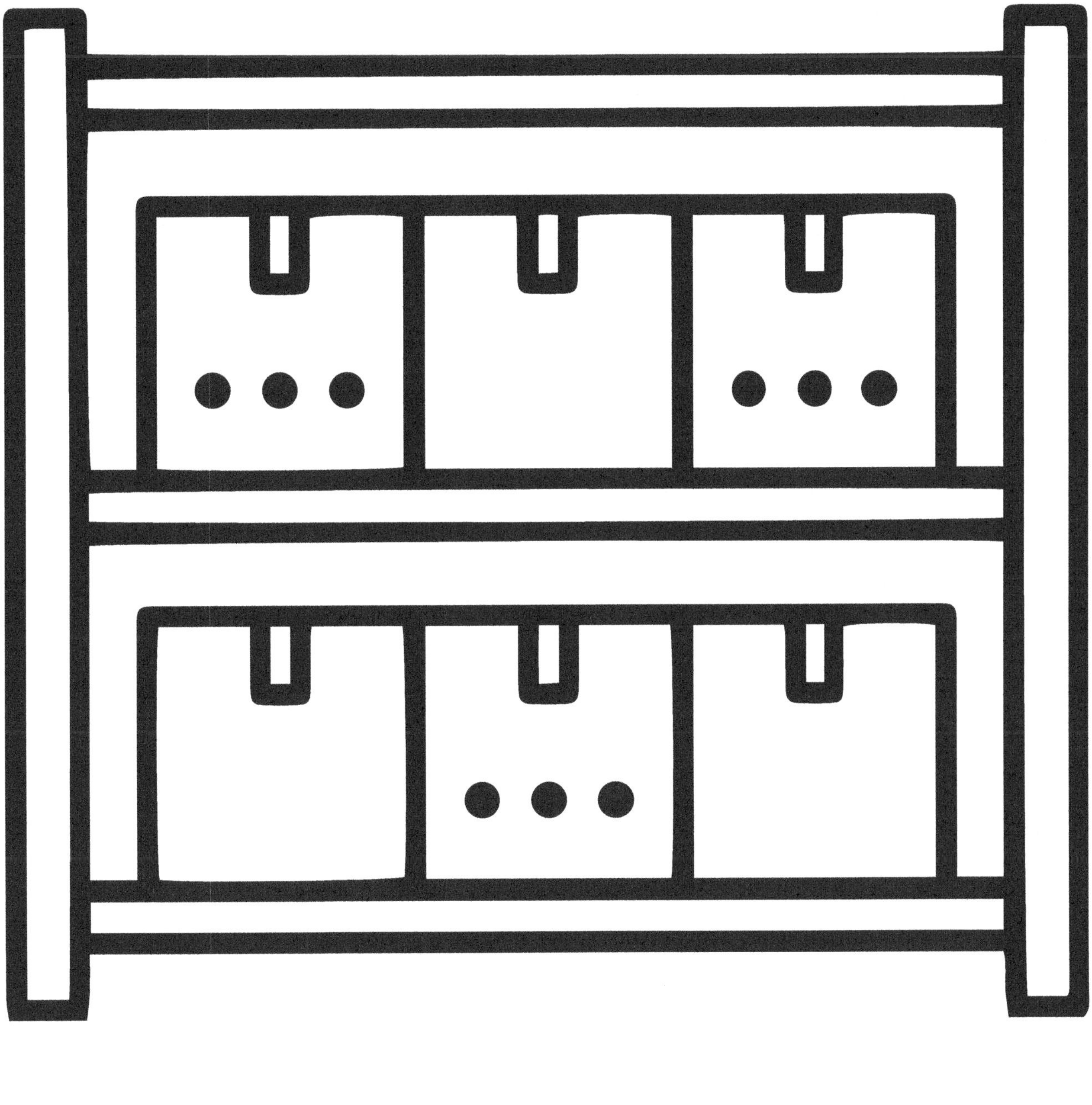

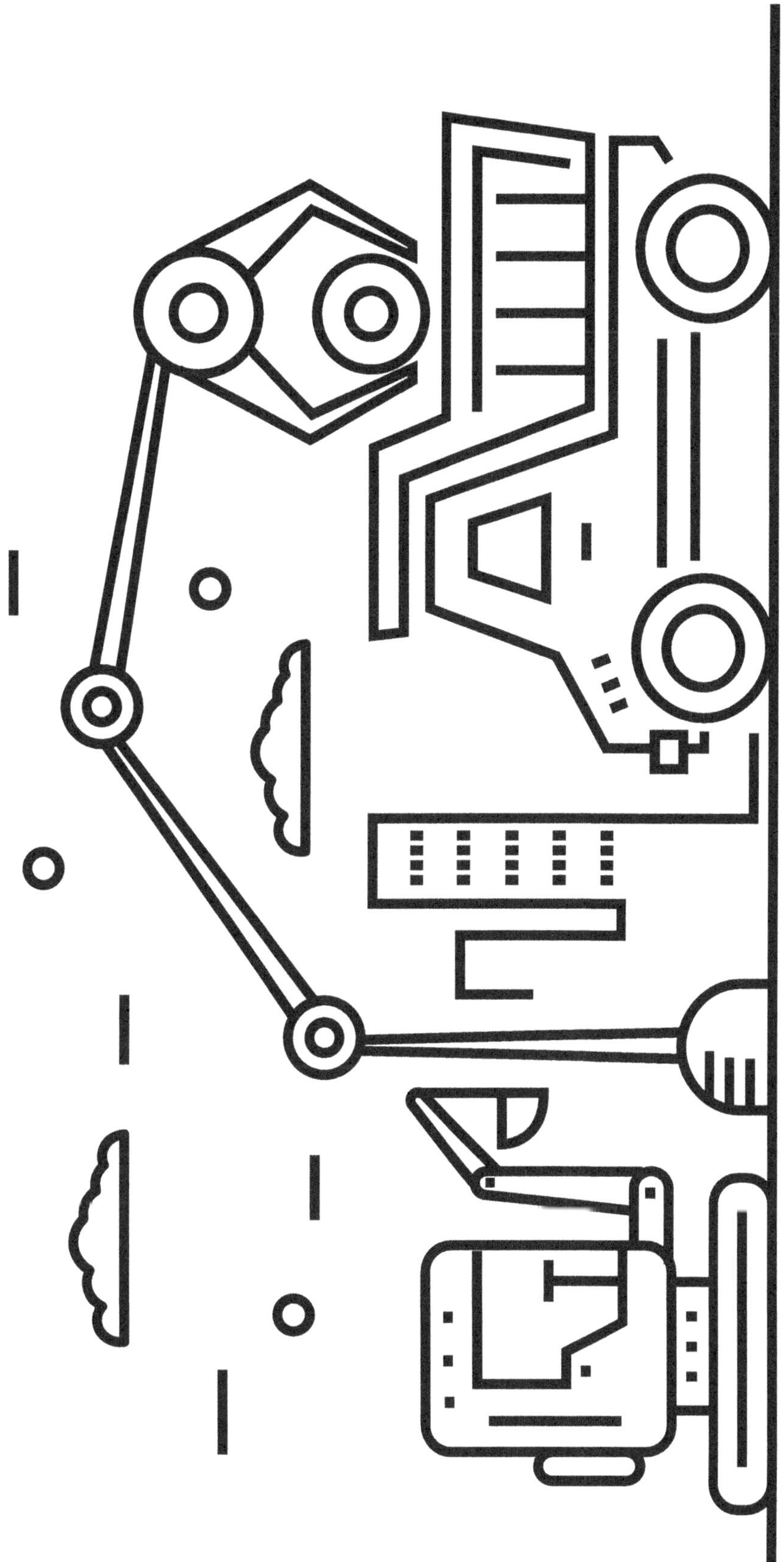

STOP

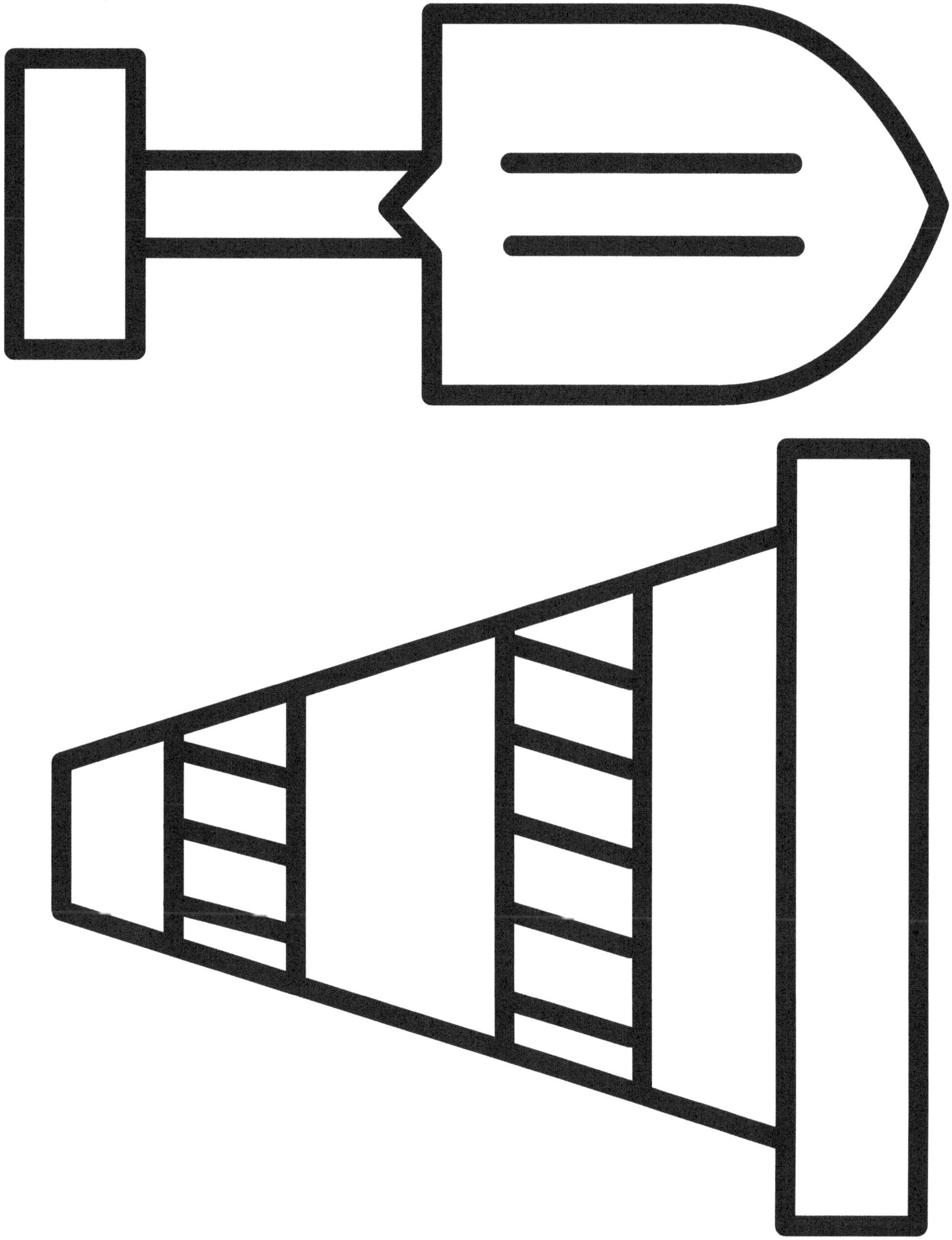

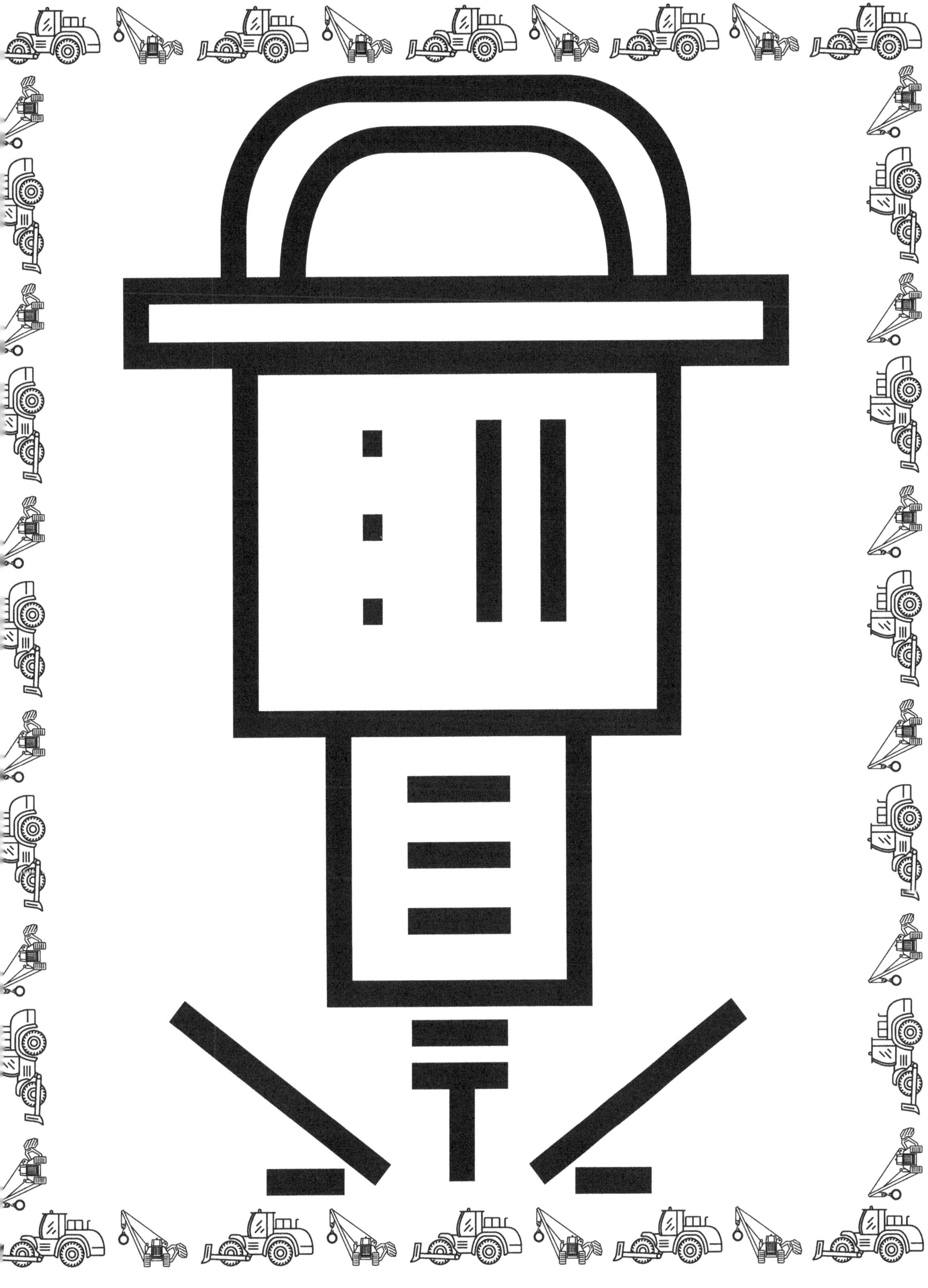

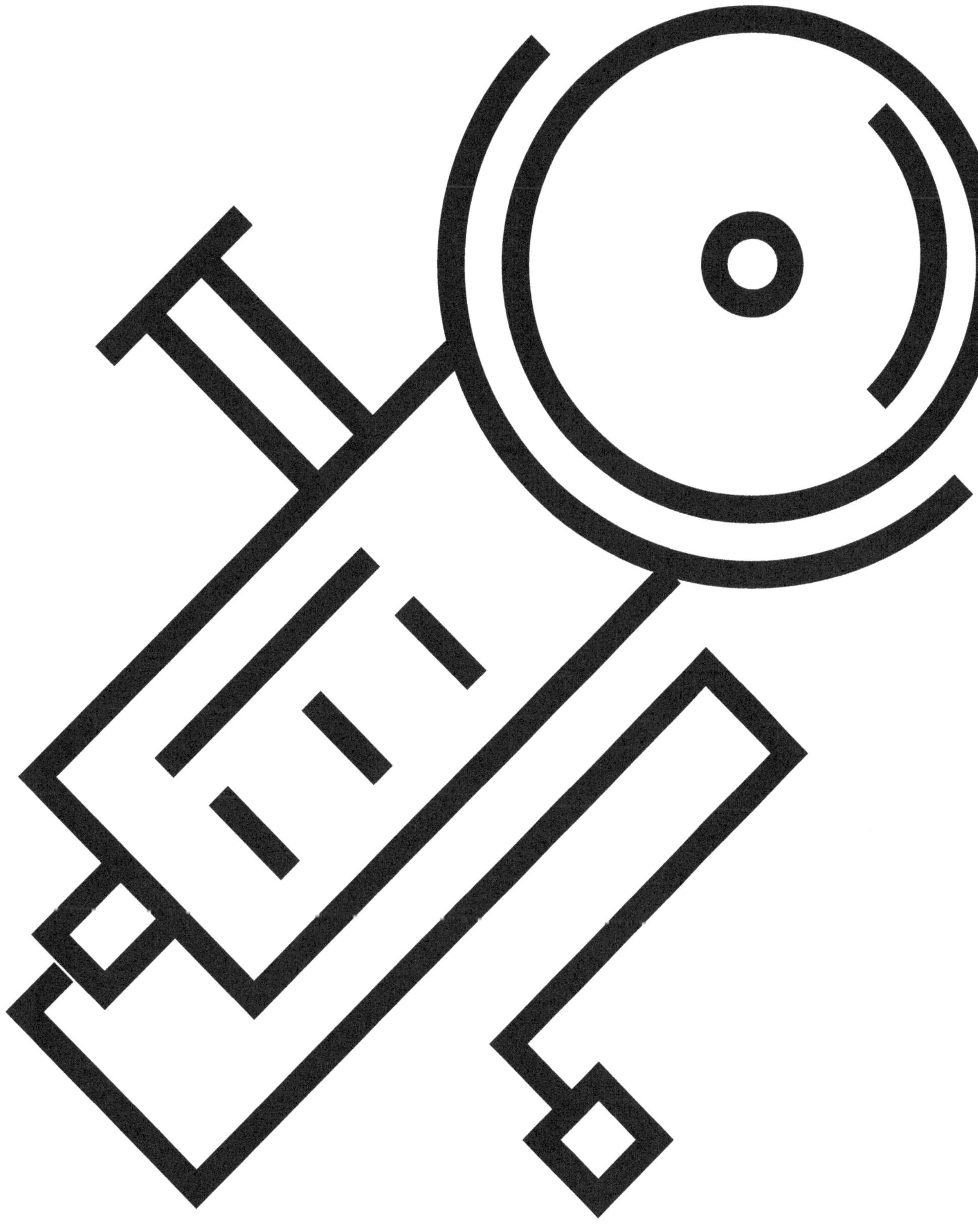

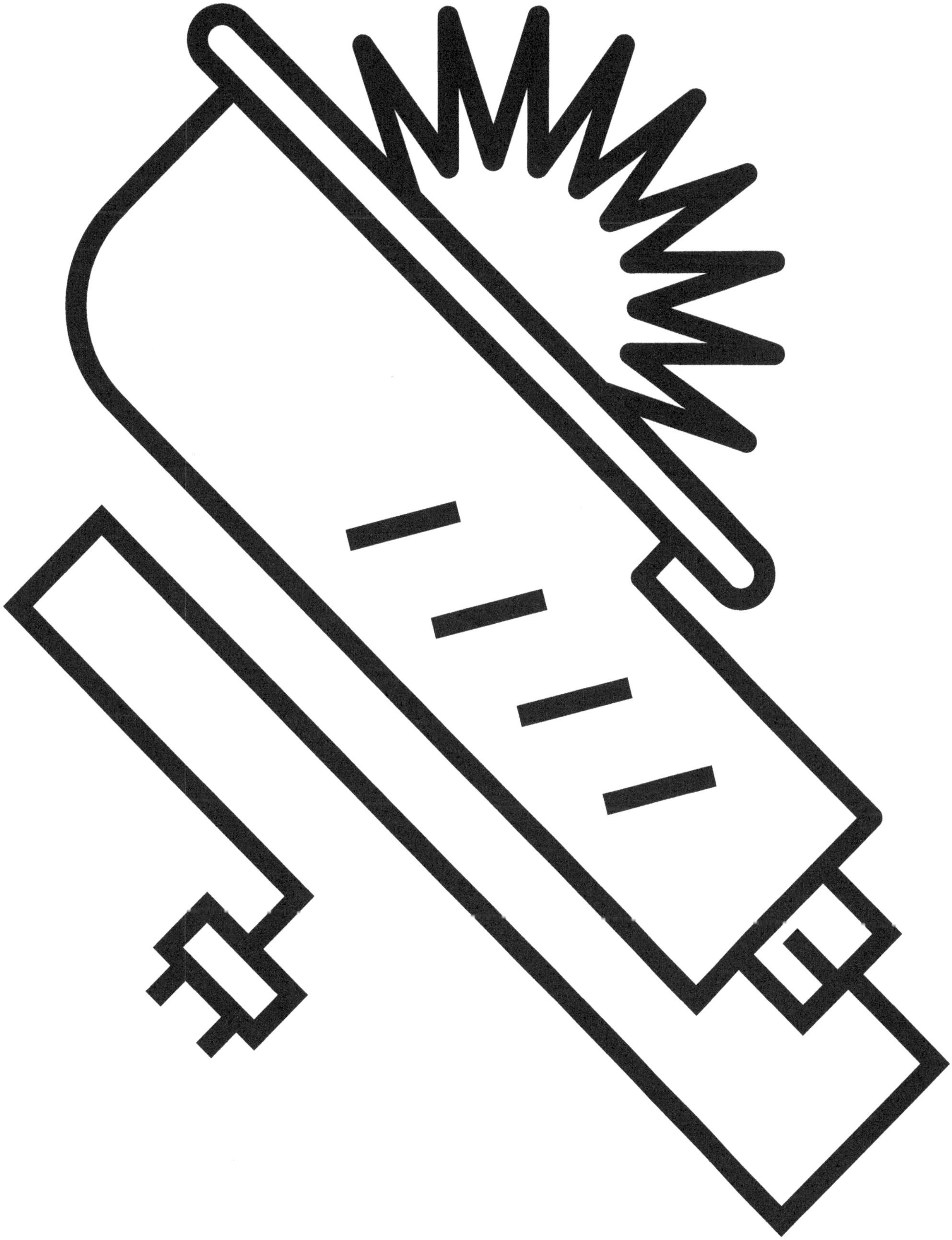

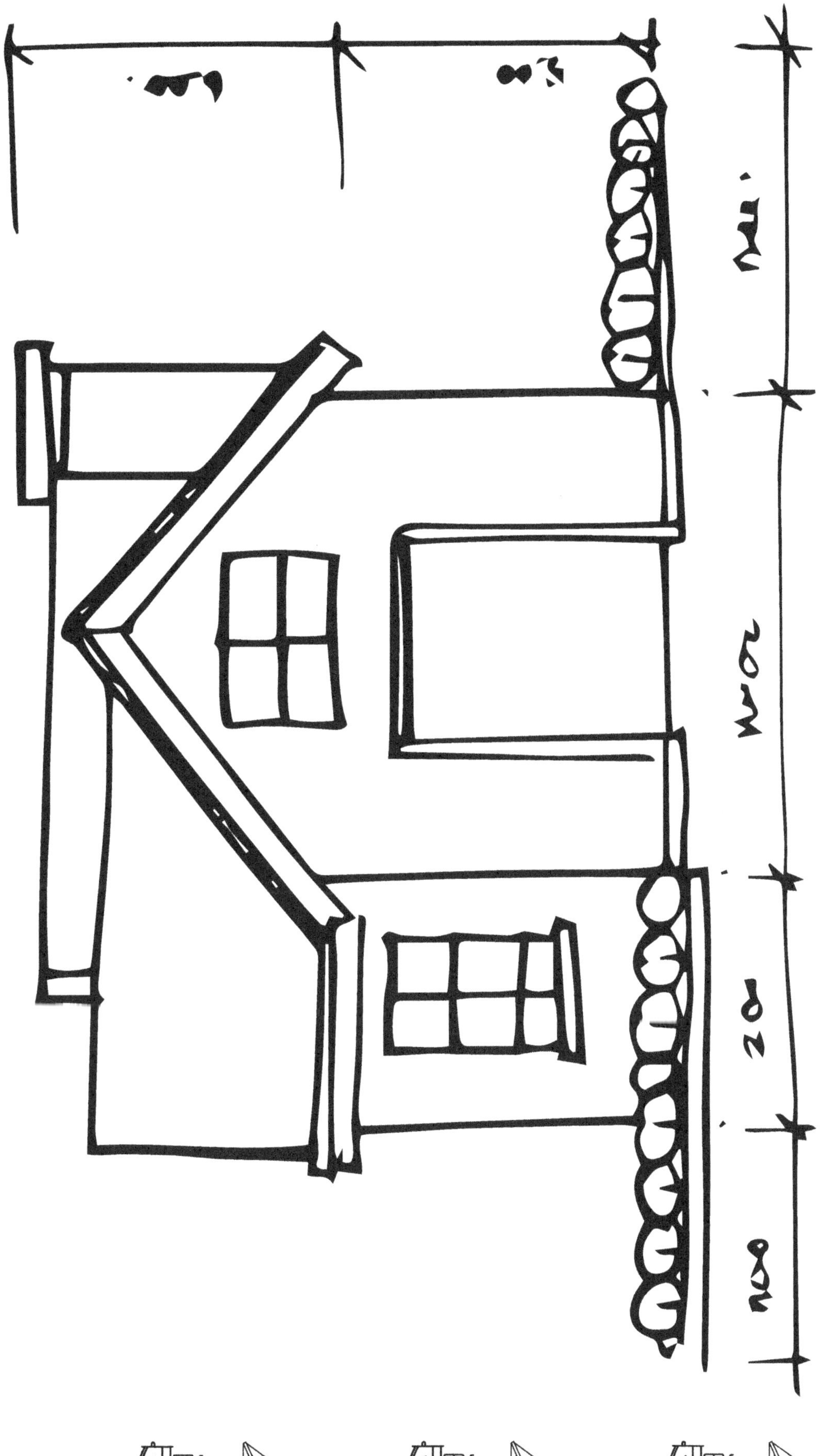

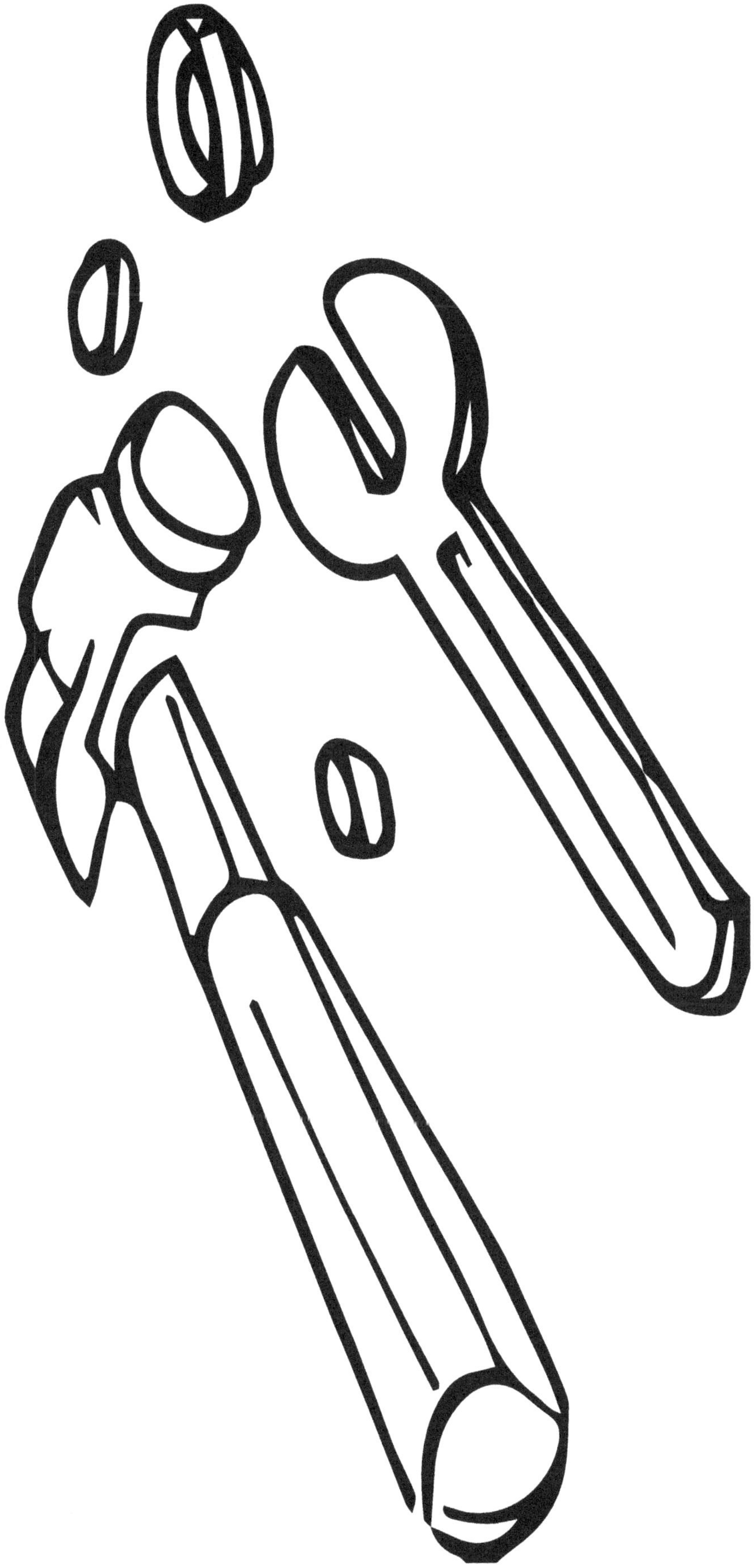

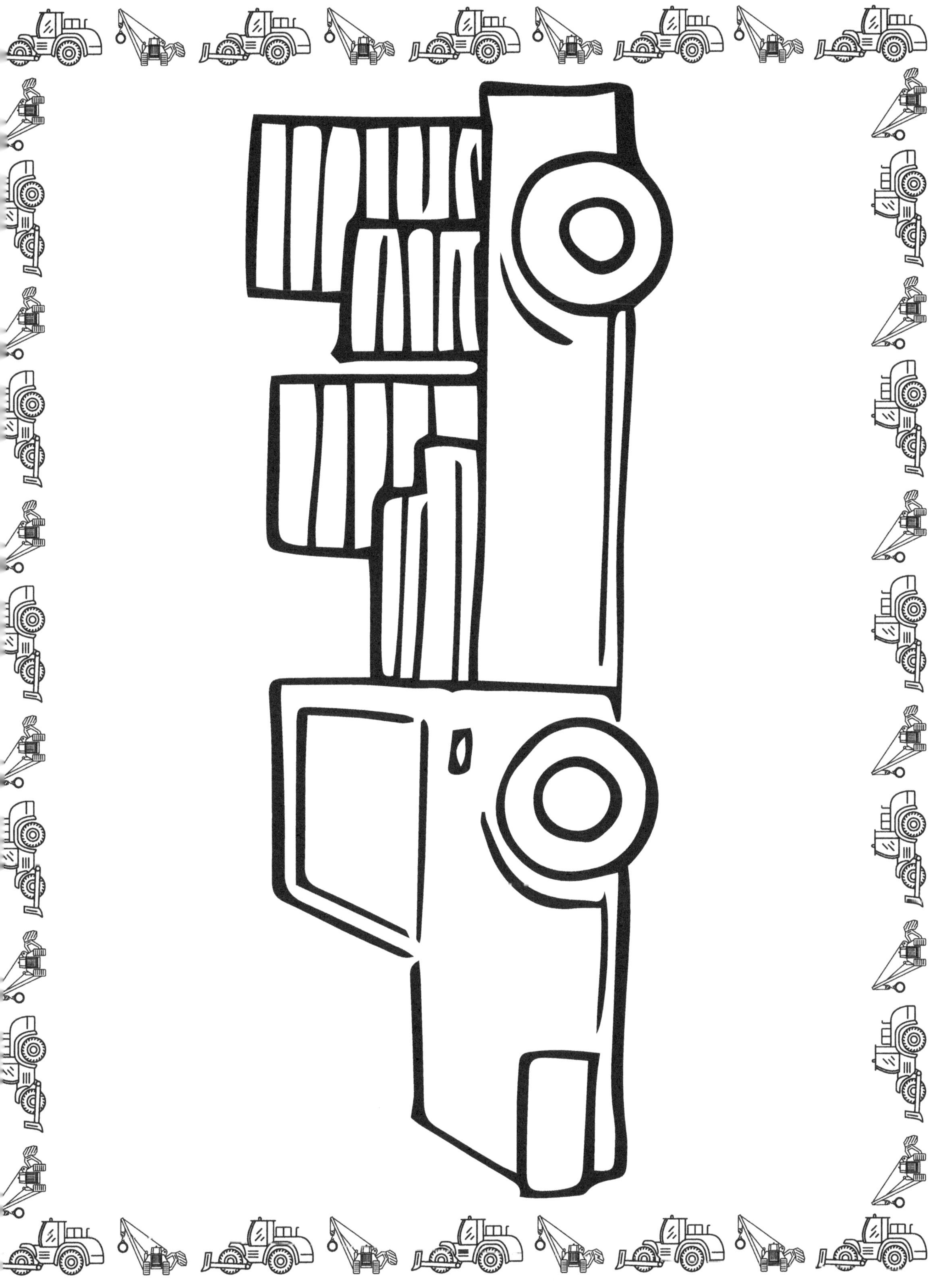

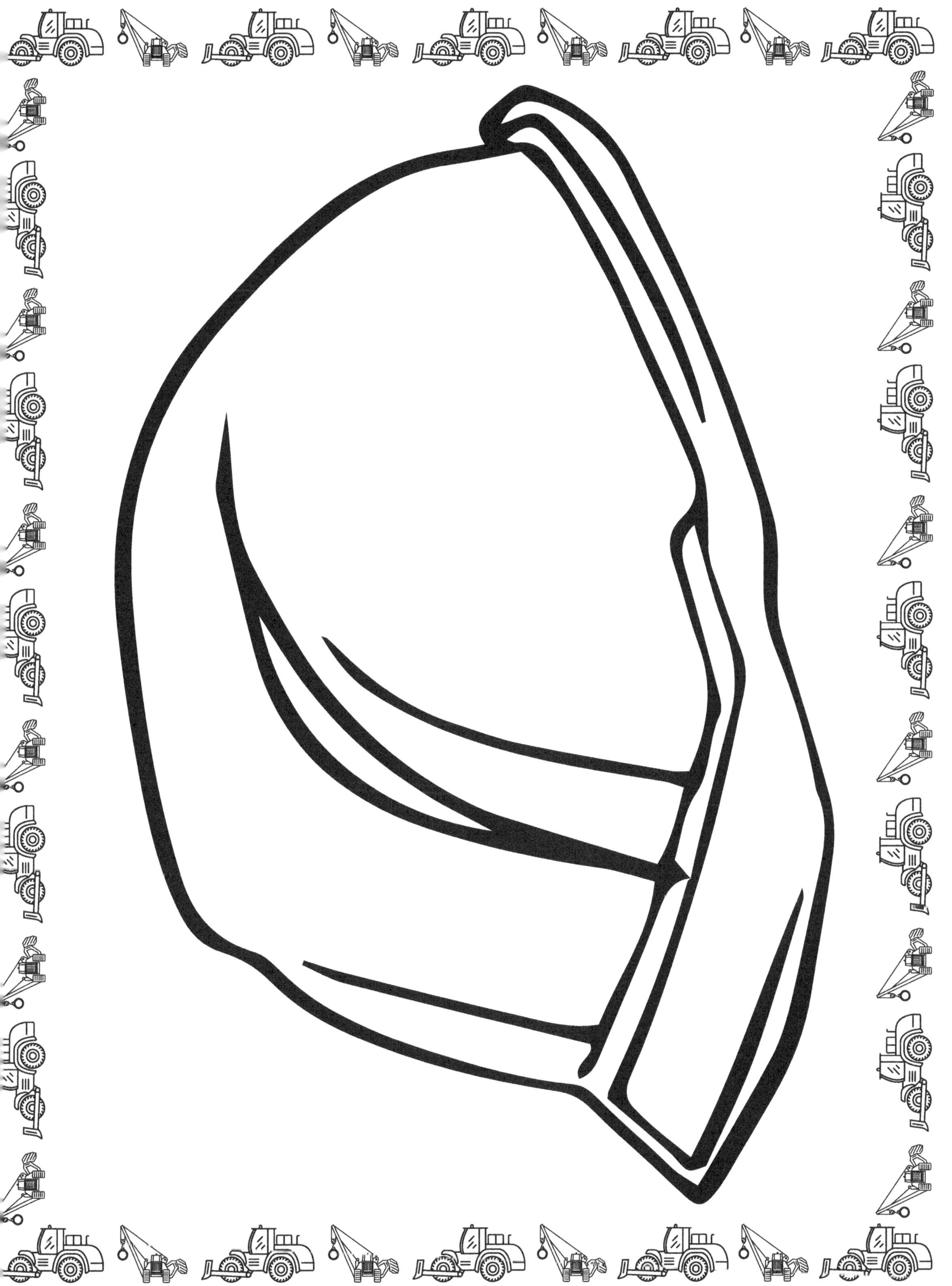

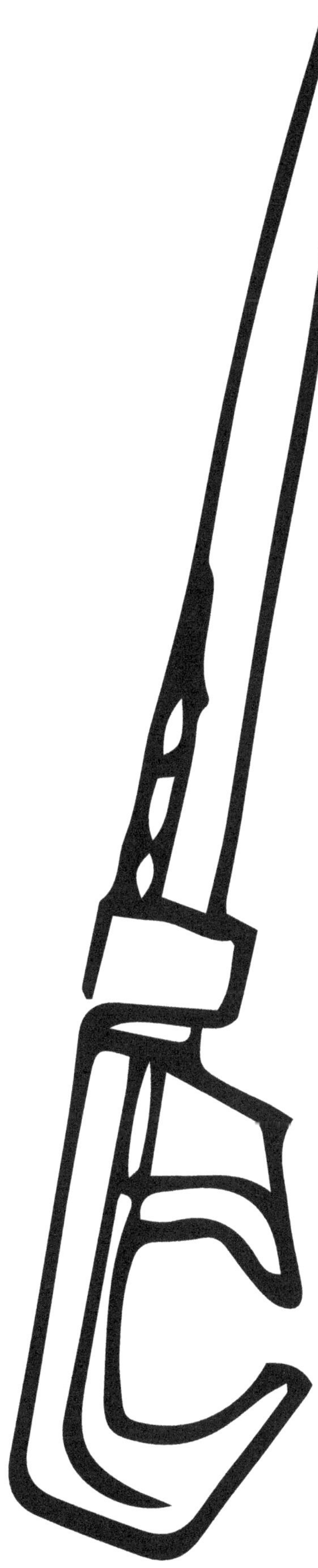

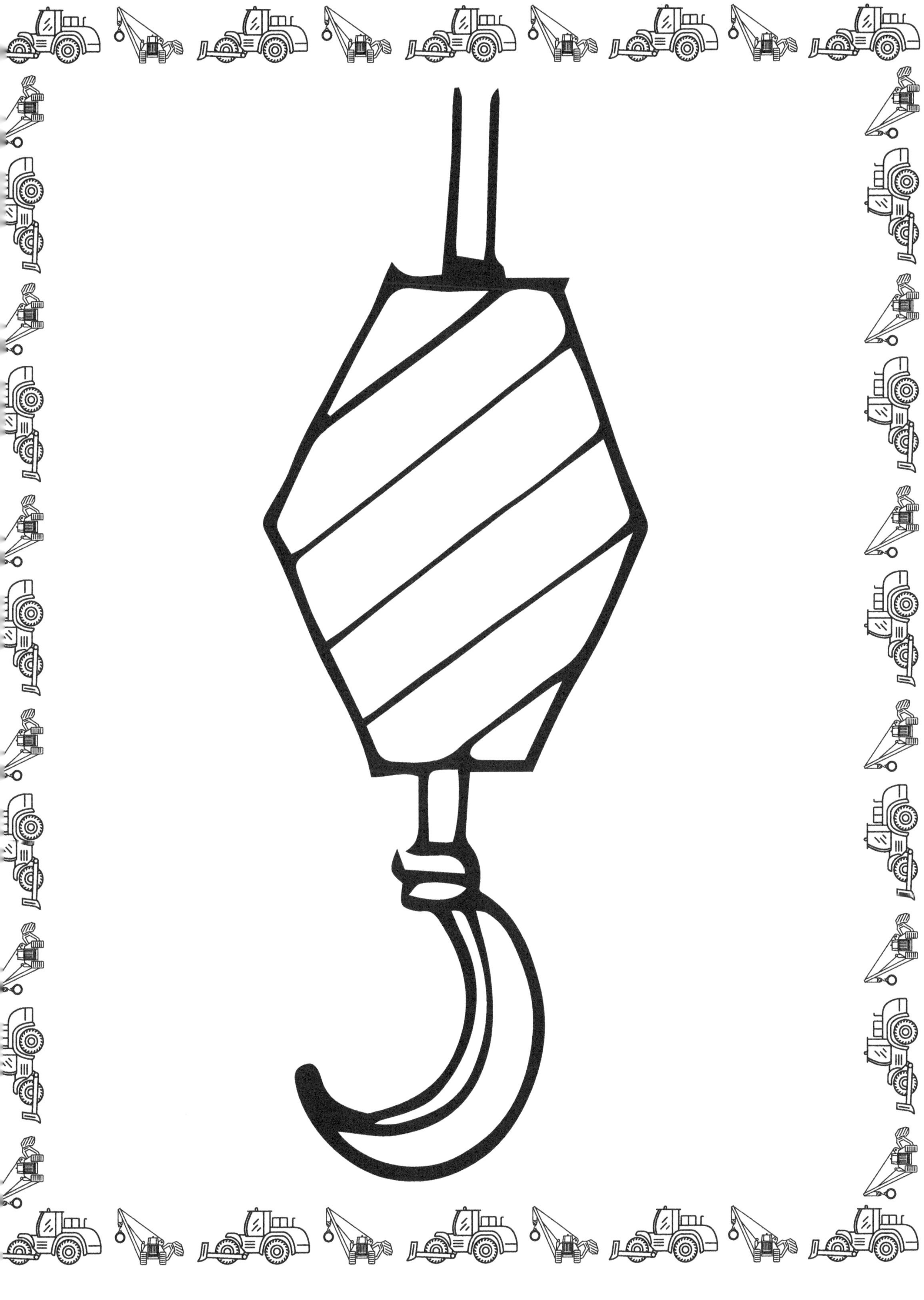

Made in the USA
Monee, IL
11 July 2020

36417740R00072